5TH GRADE US HISTORY FAMOUS US AUTHORS

An author is the originator
of any written work and can
also be described as a writer.

MARK
TWAIN

was an American author and humorist. He wrote The Adventures of Tom Sawyer and its sequel, Adventures of Huckleberry Finn. Mark Twain grew up in Hannibal, Missouri, which provided the setting for Huckleberry Finn and Tom Sawyer.

EDGAR ALLAN POE

was an American author, poet, editor, and literary critic, considered part of the American Romantic Movement. Poe was one of the earliest American practitioners of the short story, and is generally considered the inventor of the detective fiction genre.

F. SCOTT FITZGERALD

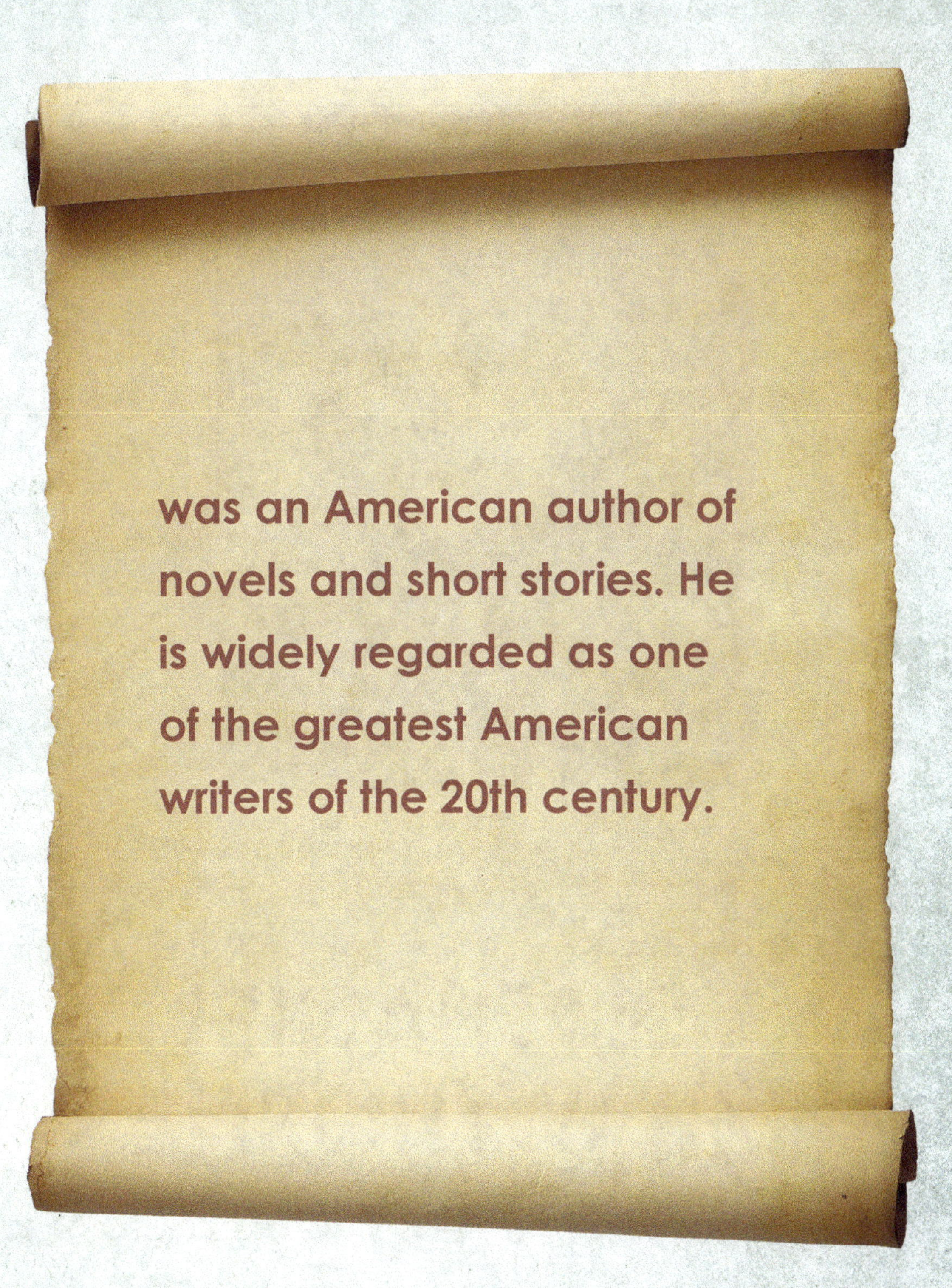

was an American author of
novels and short stories. He
is widely regarded as one
of the greatest American
writers of the 20th century.

NATHANIEL HAWTHORNE

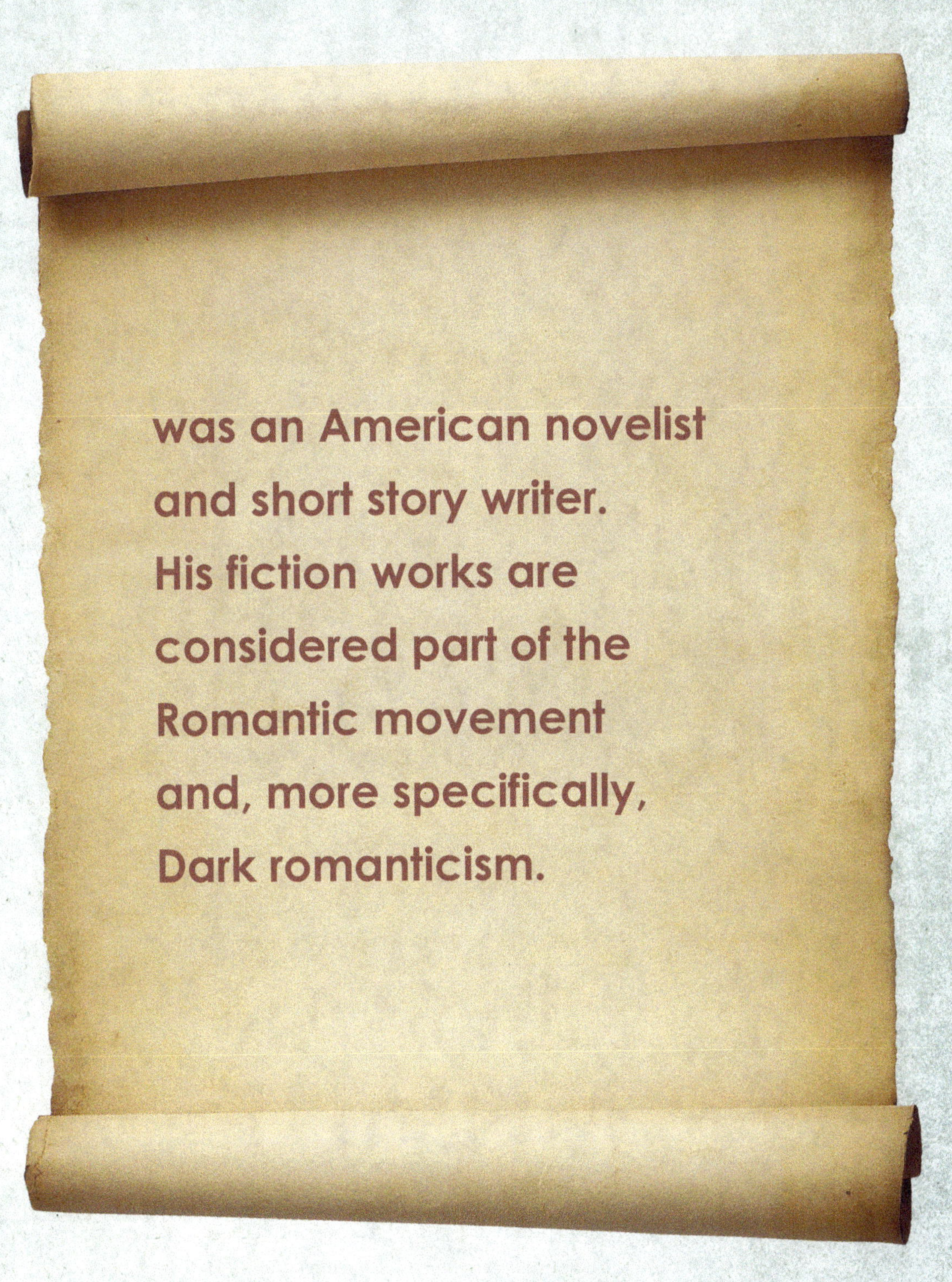

was an American novelist
and short story writer.
His fiction works are
considered part of the
Romantic movement
and, more specifically,
Dark romanticism.

HERMAN
MELVILLE

was an American novelist, writer of short stories, and poet from the American Renaissance period. Best known for his sea adventure Typee and his whaling novel Moby-Dick.

RALPH WALDO EMERSON

was an American essayist,
lecturer, and poet. He led the
Transcendentalist movement
of the mid-19th century.
His works influenced many
thinkers and philosophers.

WASHINGTON IRVING

was an American author, essayist, biographer, historian, and diplomat of the early 19th century. He is best known for his short stories "Rip Van Winkle" and "The Legend of Sleepy Hollow".

BENJAMIN FRANKLIN

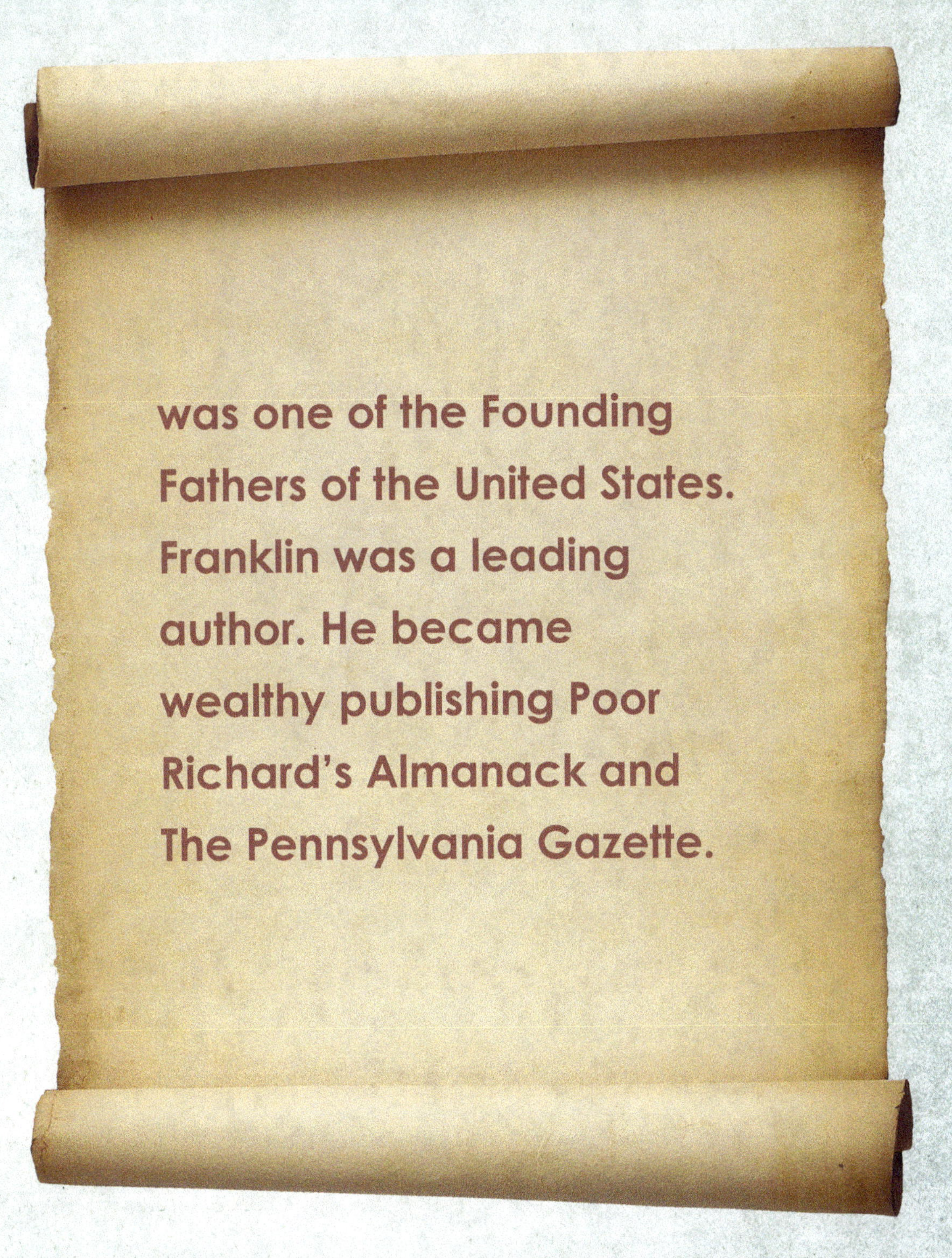

was one of the Founding
Fathers of the United States.
Franklin was a leading
author. He became
wealthy publishing Poor
Richard's Almanack and
The Pennsylvania Gazette.

HENRY DAVID THOREAU

was an American author, poet, philosopher, abolitionist, naturalist, tax resister, development critic, surveyor, and historian. Thoreau's books, articles, essays, journals, and poetry total over 20 volumes.

HARRIET BEECHER STOWE

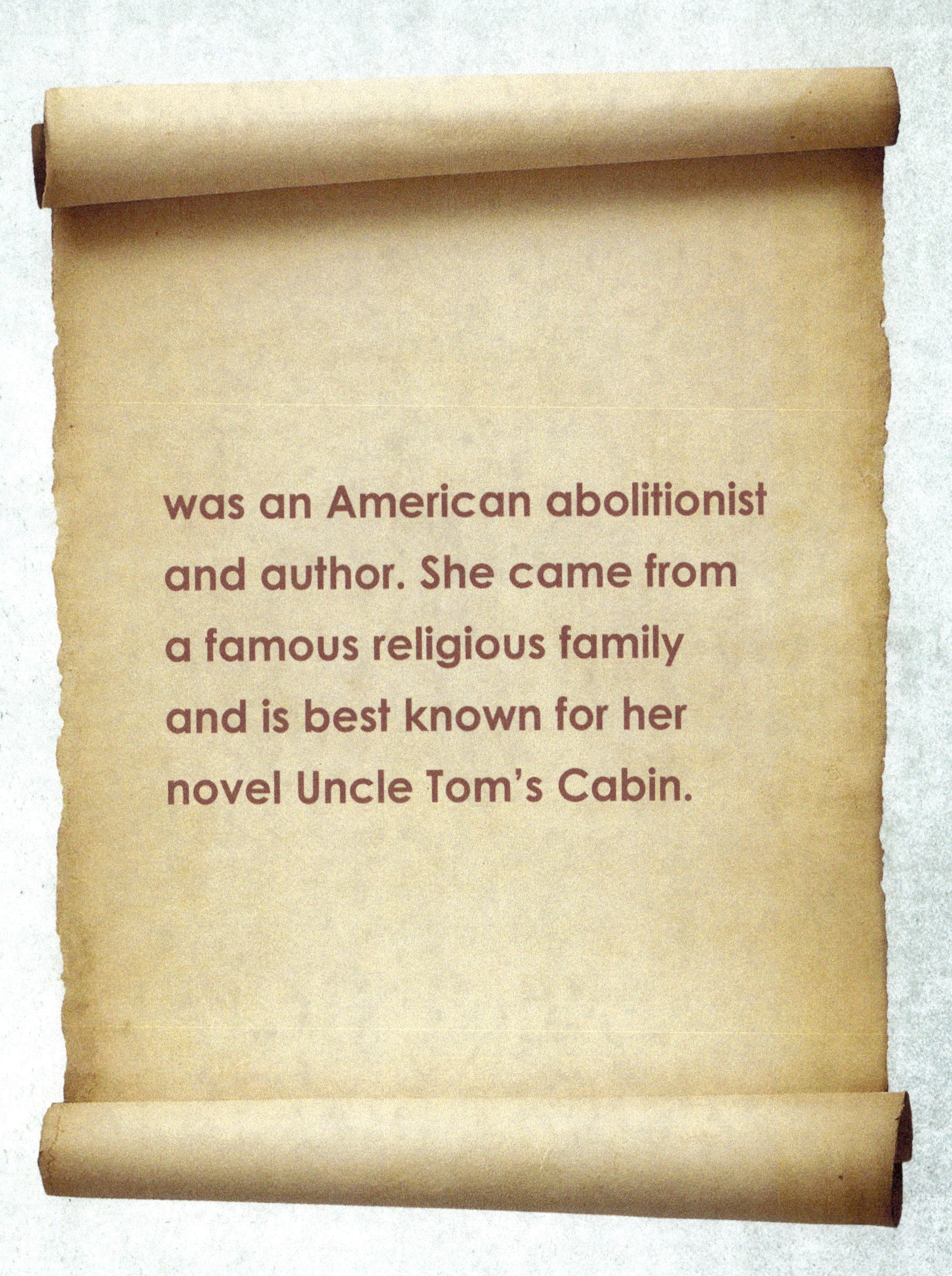

was an American abolitionist
and author. She came from
a famous religious family
and is best known for her
novel Uncle Tom's Cabin.

FREDERICK DOUGLASS

was an African-American
social reformer, abolitionist,
orator, writer, and statesman.
He described his experiences
as a slave in his 1845
autobiography, Narrative of
the Life of Frederick Douglass,
an American Slave, which
became a bestseller.

WALT
WHITMAN

was an American poet, essayist and journalist. Early in his career, he also produced a temperance novel, Franklin Evans. Whitman is among the most influential poets in the American canon, often called the father of free verse.

JAMES RUSSELL LOWELL

was an American Romantic poet, critic, editor, and diplomat. He gained notoriety in 1848 with the publication of A Fable for Critics, a book-length poem satirizing contemporary critics and poets.

OLIVER WENDELL HOLMES, SR.

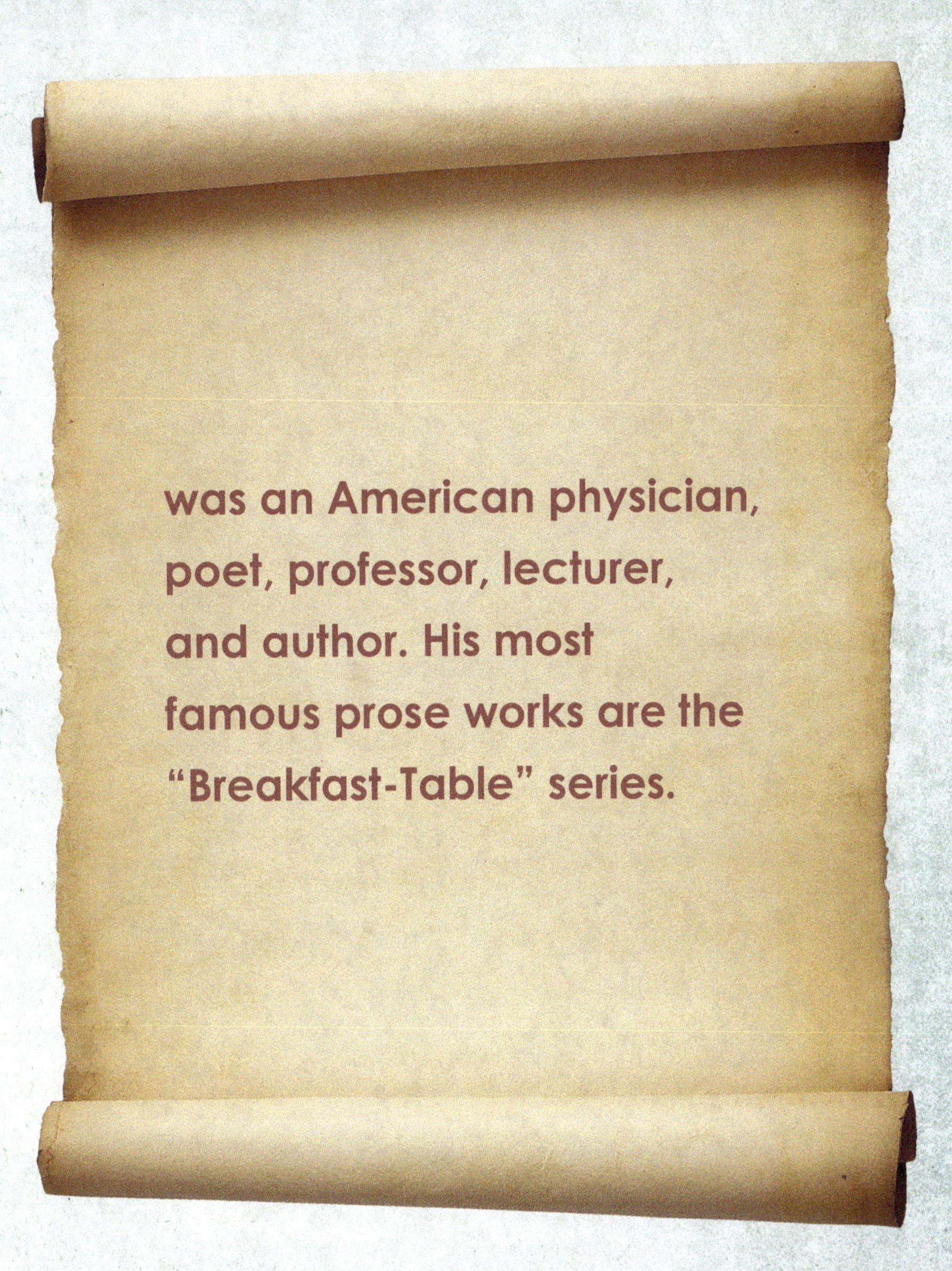
was an American physician,
poet, professor, lecturer,
and author. His most
famous prose works are the
"Breakfast-Table" series.